GRAPHIC BIOGRAPHIES

Jackie
ROBINSON
Baseball's Great Pioneer

by Jason Glaser
illustrated by Bob Lentz

Consultant:
James L. Gates Jr., Library Director
National Baseball Hall of Fame and Museum
Cooperstown, New York

Capstone
press

Mankato, Minnesota

Graphic Library is published by Capstone Press,
151 Good Counsel Drive, P.O. Box 669, Mankato, Minnesota 56002.
www.capstonepress.com

Printed in the United States of America

1 2 3 4 5 6 10 09 08 07 06 05

Library of Congress Cataloging-in-Publication Data
Glaser, Jason.
Jackie Robinson, baseball's great pioneer / by Jason Glaser; illustrated by Bob Lentz.
p. cm.—(Graphic library. Graphic biographies)
Summary: "In graphic novel format, tells the life story of Jackie Robinson and his pro baseball career"—Provided by publisher.
Includes bibliographical references and index.
ISBN-13: 978-0-7368-4633-2 (hardcover)
ISBN-10: 0-7368-4633-6 (hardcover)
ISBN-13: 978-0-7368-6197-7 (softcover pbk.)
ISBN-10: 0-7368-6197-1 (softcover pbk.)
1. Robinson, Jackie, 1919–1972—Juvenile literature. 2. Baseball players—United States—Biography—Juvenile literature. I. Lentz, Bob, ill. II. Title. III. Series.
GV865.R6G53 2006
796.357'092—dc22 2005003345

Art Director and Designer
Bob Lentz

Editor
Tom Adamson

Editor's note: Direct quotations from primary sources are indicated by a yellow background.

Direct quotations appear on the following pages:
Pages 11, 25, quoted in *Great Time Coming* by David Falkner (New York: Simon and Schuster, 1995).
Pages 13, 17, 20, 22, 26, from *I Never Had It Made* by Jackie Robinson (New York: HarperCollins, 1995).
Page 18, from *Wait Till Next Year* by Carl T. Rowan with Jackie Robinson (New York: Random House, 1960).

Table of Contents

CHAPTER	TITLE	PAGE
1	GIFT OF GRACE	4
2	SERVING HIS COUNTRY	10
3	INTEGRATING BASEBALL	18
4	NEVER HAD IT MADE	24

EXTRA INNINGS

More about Jackie Robinson 28

Glossary 30

Internet Sites 30

Read More 31

Bibliography 31

Index 32

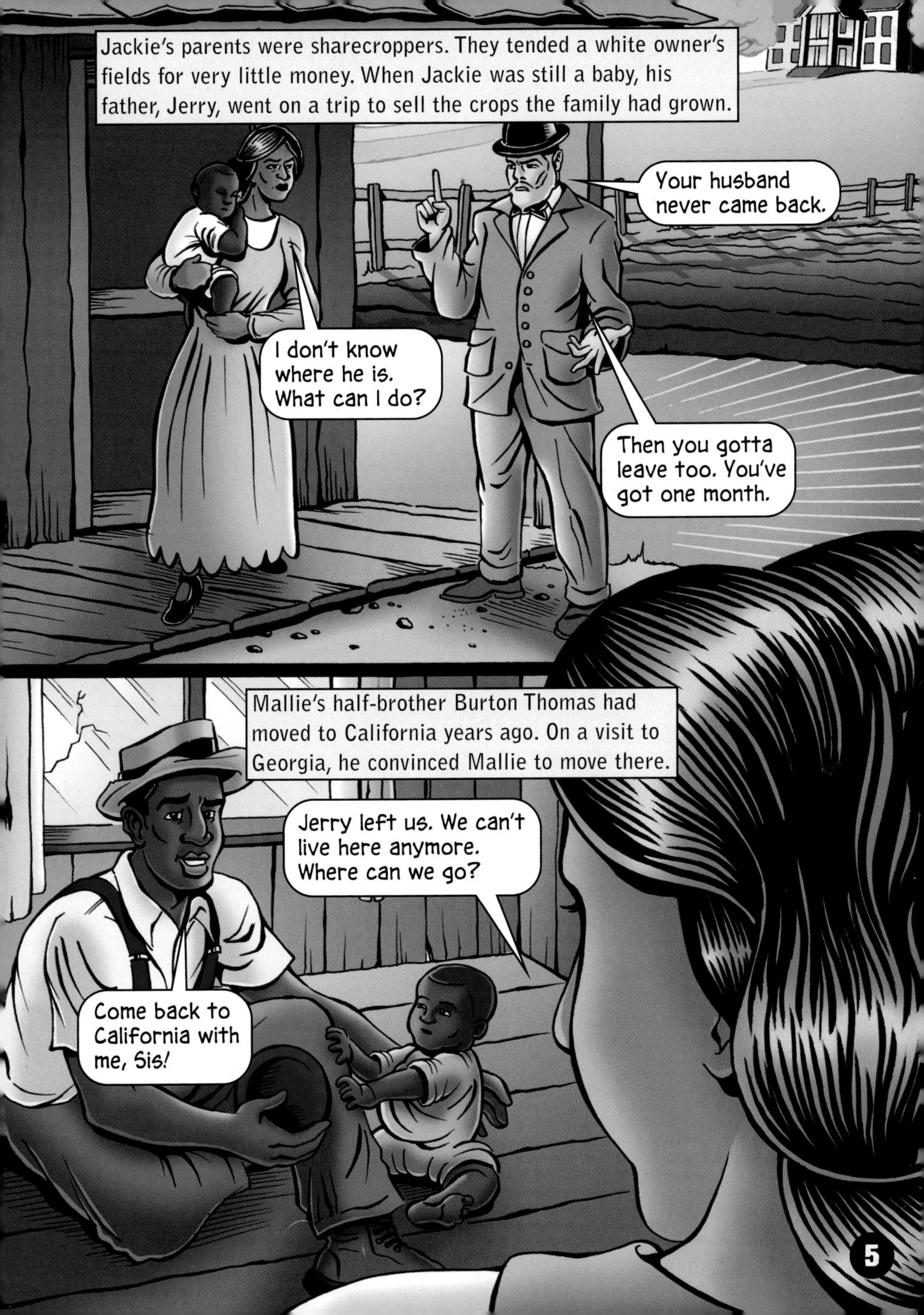
Jackie's parents were sharecroppers. They tended a white owner's fields for very little money. When Jackie was still a baby, his father, Jerry, went on a trip to sell the crops the family had grown.
Your husband never came back.
I don't know where he is. What can I do?
Then you gotta leave too. You've got one month.
Mallie's half-brother Burton Thomas had moved to California years ago. On a visit to Georgia, he convinced Mallie to move there.
Jerry left us. We can't live here anymore. Where can we go?
Come back to California with me, Sis!

In 1920, Jackie's family moved to Pasadena, California. Mallie hoped her children would have more freedom and opportunity. By age 8, Jackie was a graceful athlete.

C'mon, hit him!

I'm trying!

He's too quick!

Great shot, Jack*! You've got a good arm.

CRASSHHH!!

As a teenager, Jackie joined a group of boys known as the Pepper Street Gang. They vandalized cars, signs, and lights in their neighborhood. Jackie was trying to fit in with the other neighborhood boys.

You darkies get away from here!

Darkies?! Let's tar his lawn tonight for that.

* The world came to know him as Jackie. But most everyone who knew him called him Jack.

After two years at UCLA, Jackie decided that a college degree was not going to help him get a job. African Americans had a hard time getting good-paying jobs. The only way Jackie felt he could get ahead in a segregated America was through sports.

Touchdown! Robinson puts up six for the College All-Stars!

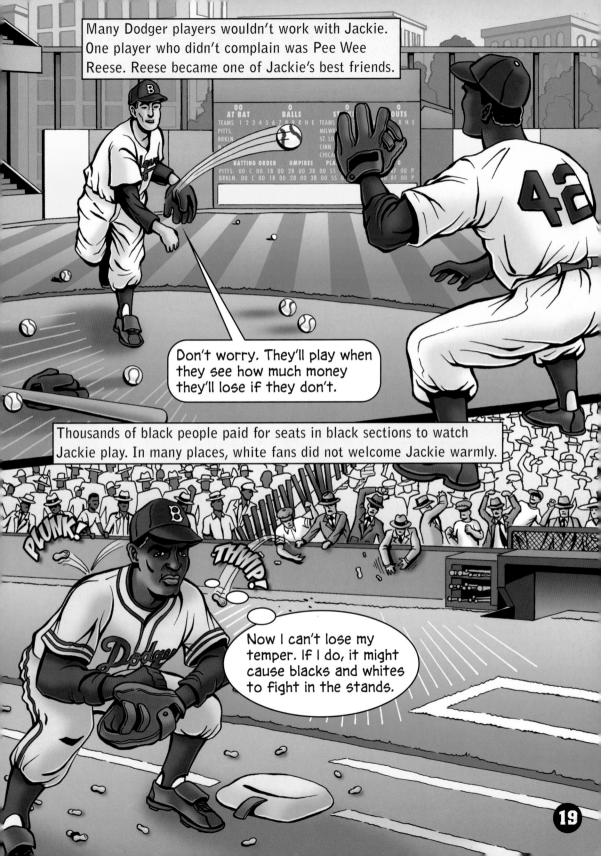

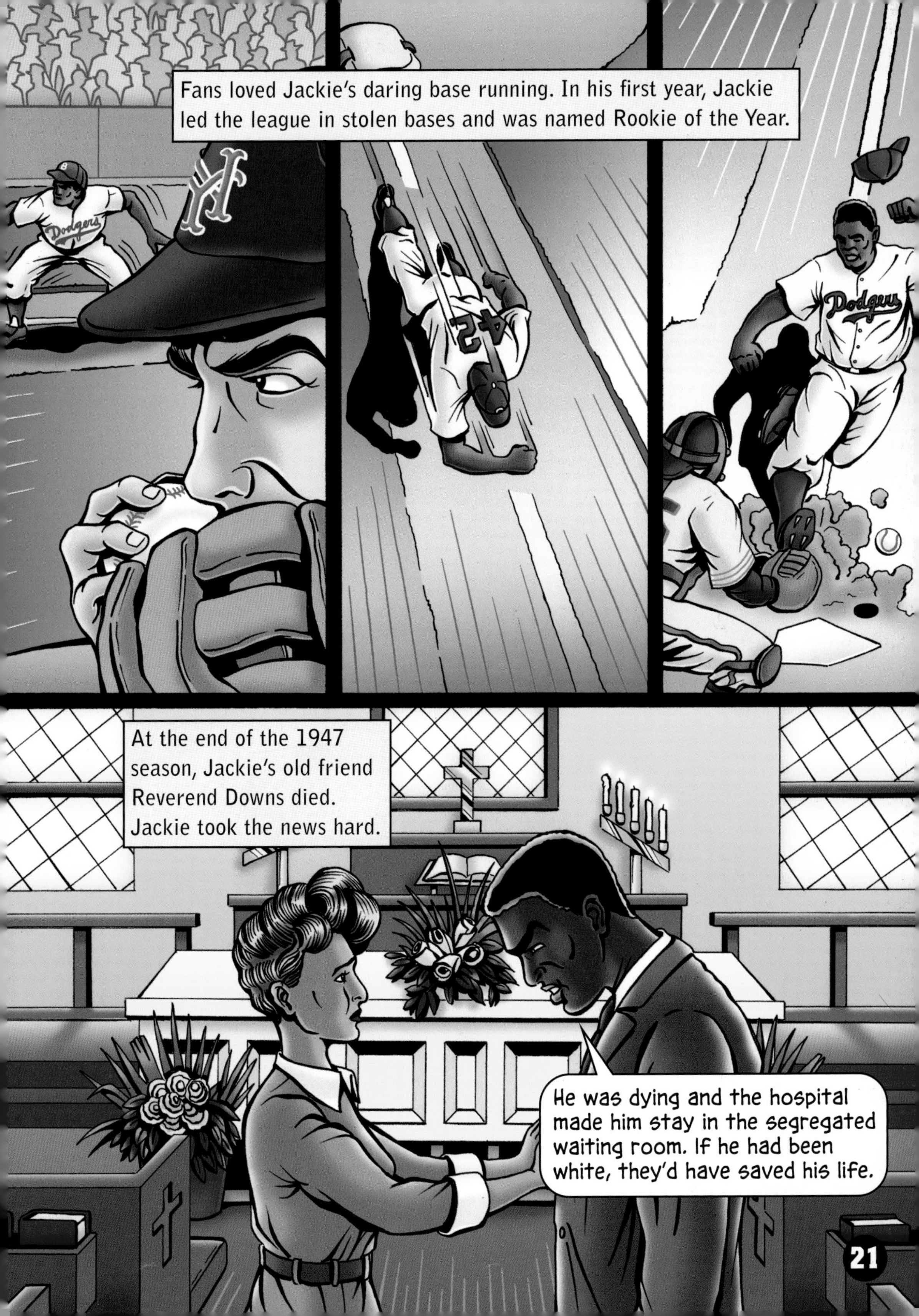

Fans loved Jackie's daring base running. In his first year, Jackie led the league in stolen bases and was named Rookie of the Year.
At the end of the 1947 season, Jackie's old friend Reverend Downs died. Jackie took the news hard.
He was dying and the hospital made him stay in the segregated waiting room. If he had been white, they'd have saved his life.

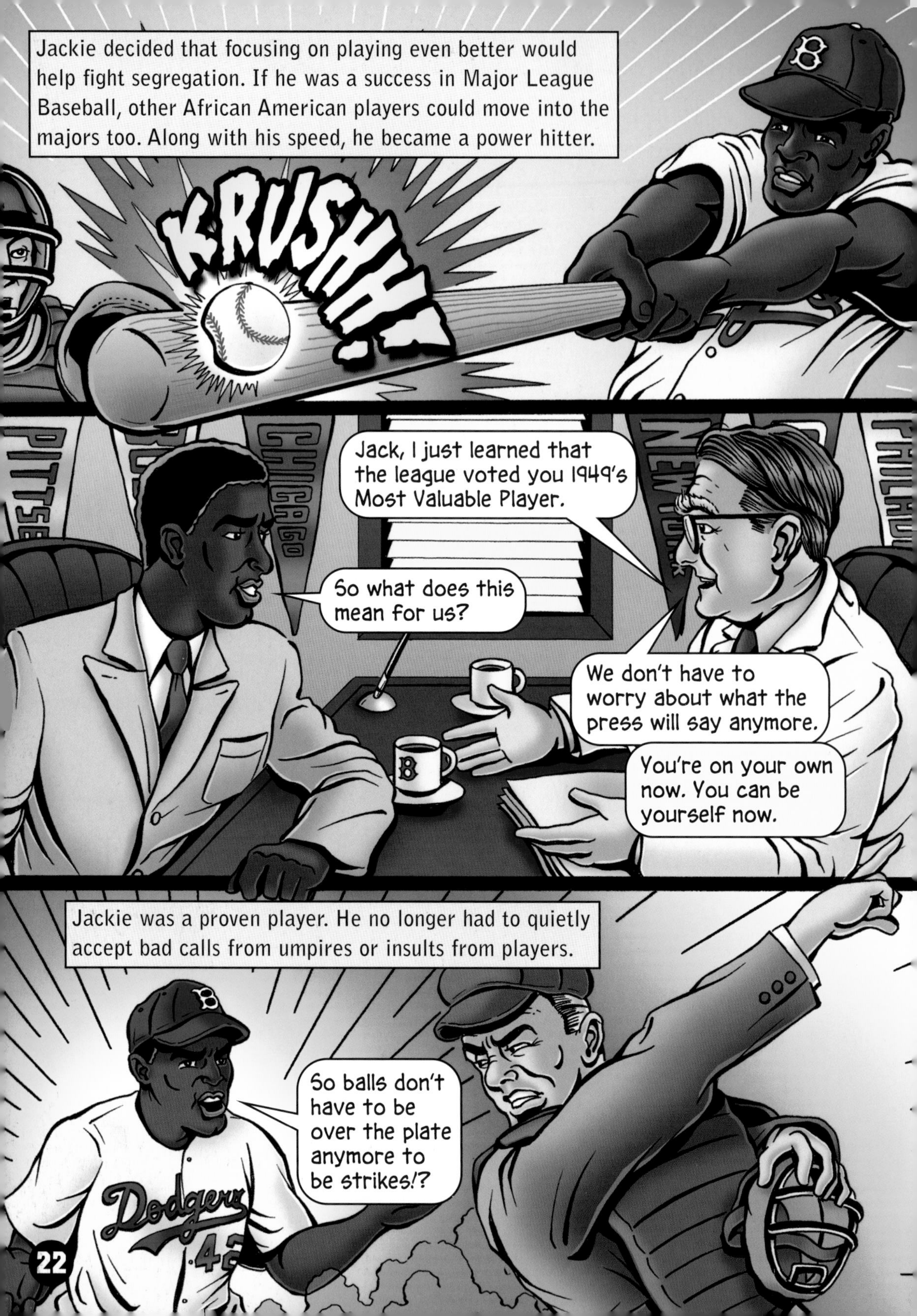
Jackie decided that focusing on playing even better would help fight segregation. If he was a success in Major League Baseball, other African American players could move into the majors too. Along with his speed, he became a power hitter.
KRUSH!
CHICAGO
Jack, I just learned that the league voted you 1949's Most Valuable Player.
So what does this mean for us?
We don't have to worry about what the press will say anymore.
You're on your own now. You can be yourself now.
Jackie was a proven player. He no longer had to quietly accept bad calls from umpires or insults from players.
So balls don't have to be over the plate anymore to be strikes!?
Dodgers
42

JACKIE ROOSEVELT ROBINSON

BORN: January 31, 1919, Cairo, Georgia
HEIGHT: 5' 11" **WEIGHT:** 204 lbs
BATS: Right **THROWS:** Right

42

BROOKLYN DODGERS

Year	G	R	H	HR	RBI	SB	Avg
1947	151	125	175	12	48	29	.297
1948	147	108	170	12	85	22	.296
1949	156	122	203	16	124	37	.342
1950	144	99	170	14	81	12	.328
1951	153	106	185	19	88	25	.338
1952	149	104	157	19	75	24	.308
1953	136	109	159	12	95	17	.329
1954	124	62	120	15	59	7	.311
1955	105	51	81	8	36	12	.256
1956	117	61	98	10	43	12	.275
Career	1,382	947	1,518	137	734	197	.311

KEY:
G = Games
R = Runs
H = Hits
HR = Home runs
RBI = Runs batted in
SB = Stolen bases
Avg = Batting average

More about JACKIE ROBINSON

- Jack Roosevelt Robinson was born January 31, 1919.

- Jackie's middle name, Roosevelt, was given in honor of President Theodore Roosevelt. Roosevelt was against segregation. He died just before Jackie was born.

- A movie about Jackie, *The Jackie Robinson Story*, was made while he was still playing baseball. The movie studio needed a black actor who could run and hit well. Jackie ended up playing himself in the movie.

- Sometimes when Jackie was on base, a ball would get hit nearby that looked like it might result in a double play. Jackie would "accidentally" let the ball hit him as he ran between bases. This move would usually ruin the double play. The league saw this strategy as unfair, so it added a new rule. If a runner is struck by a hit ball, the runner and the batter are both out. This rule is sometimes called the "Jackie Robinson rule."

- In 1957, the new owner of the Brooklyn Dodgers moved the team to Los Angeles, California.

- Jackie was crucial to the integration of pro sports, but he was not the first black man to play pro baseball. Moses Fleetwood Walker played catcher for the American Association in 1884.

- Jackie excelled at every sport he ever played except one. While vacationing in the Catskill Mountains in New York, Jackie tried skiing. He fell down several times and gave up on skiing forever.

- Jackie and Rachel had three children: Jackie Jr., Sharon, and David. In 1971, Jackie Jr. was killed in a car accident at age 24, a little more than one year before Jackie died.

- To honor a former player, baseball teams sometimes retire a player's number. That number will never be worn by another player of the team. In 1997, Jackie's number 42 was retired from all of Major League Baseball.

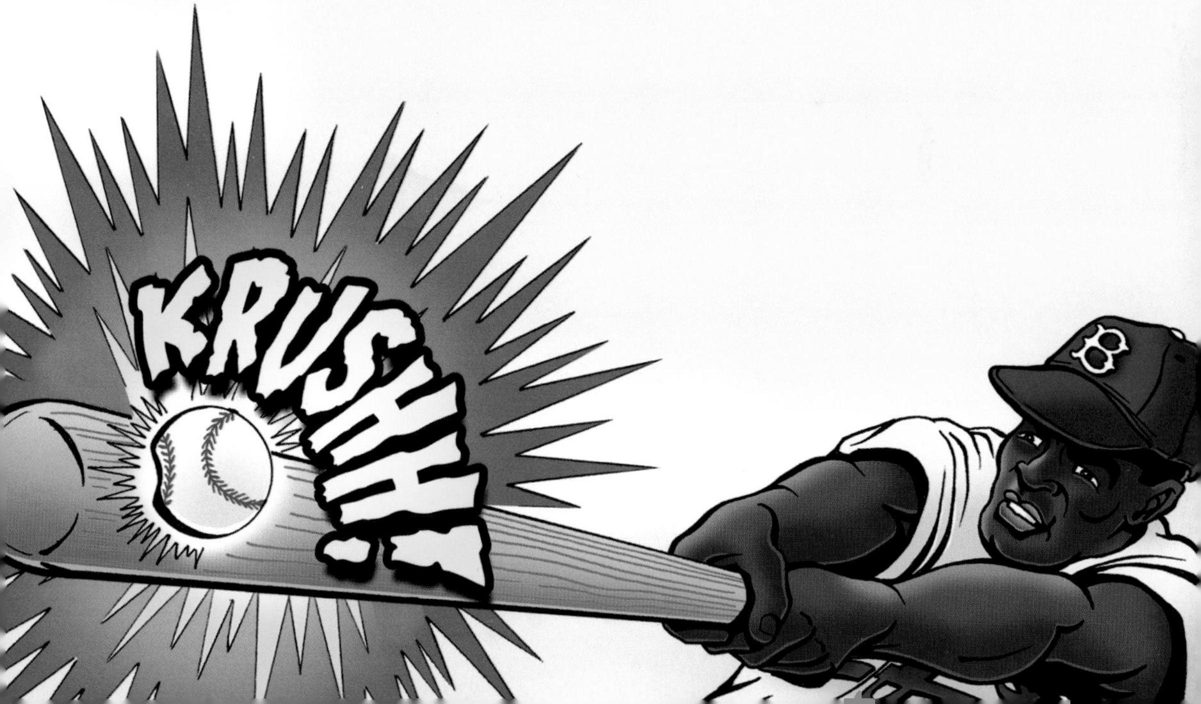
KRUSH!

GLOSSARY

court-martial (KORT-mar-shuhl)—to send someone to a military trial

draft (DRAFT)—to require to enlist in the military

morale (muh-RAL)—a person or group's feelings or state of mind

regulations (reg-yuh-LAY-shuhns)—official rules

reverend (REV-ruhnd)—the leader of a church

segregation (seg-ruh-GAY-shuhn)—the act of keeping people or groups apart

sharecropper (SHAIR-krop-ur)—a person who works farm fields for an owner in exchange for a small part of the profits

vandalize (VAN-duhl-ize)—to needlessly damage property

INTERNET SITES

FactHound offers a safe, fun way to find Internet sites related to this book. All of the sites on FactHound have been researched by our staff.

Here's how:

1. *Visit www.facthound.com*
2. Type in this special code **0736846336** for age-appropriate sites. Or enter a search word related to this book for a more general search.
3. Click on the **Fetch It** button.

FactHound will fetch the best sites for you!

READ MORE

De Marco, Tony. *Jackie Robinson*. Chanhassen, Minn.: Child's World, 2002.

Editors of *Time for Kids*, with Denise Lewis Patrick. *Jackie Robinson: Strong Inside and Out*. New York: HarperCollins, 2005.

Robinson, Sharon. *Promises to Keep: How Jackie Robinson Changed America*. New York: Scholastic, 2004.

Wheeler, Jill C. *Jackie Robinson*. Breaking Barriers. Edina, Minn.: Abdo, 2003.

BIBLIOGRAPHY

baseball-reference.com. Jackie Robinson. http://www.baseball-reference.com/r/robinja02.shtml.

Falkner, David. *Great Time Coming*. New York: Simon and Schuster, 1995.

Rampersad, Arnold. *Jackie Robinson*. New York: Knopf, 1997.

Robinson, Jackie. *I Never Had It Made*. New York: HarperCollins, 1995.

Robinson, Sharon. *Stealing Home: an Intimate Family Portrait by the Daughter of Jackie Robinson*. New York: HarperCollins, 1997.

Rowan, Carl T., with Jackie Robinson. *Wait Till Next Year: The Life Story of Jackie Robinson*. New York: Random House, 1960.

INDEX

Brooklyn Dodgers, 16, 18–23, 24, 28

California, 5, 6, 12
Chock Full o' Nuts, 24

Downs, Reverend Karl, 7, 17, 21

Freedom National Bank, 25

Georgia, 4–5

Kansas City Monarchs, 16

Major League Baseball, 15–16, 18–23, 29
Montreal Royals, 18

Negro League baseball, 15–16

Pearl Harbor, 12
Pepper Street Gang, 6

Reese, Pee Wee, 19
Rickey, Branch, 16–17, 22–23

Robinson, Frank (brother), 8–9
Robinson, Jackie
   in the army, 13–15
   baseball career of, 16–17, 18–23, 24, 27, 28
   birth of, 4, 28
   childhood of, 4–7
   children of, 29
   in college, 8–9, 10
   death of, 26
   and Hall of Fame, 25
   and Most Valuable Player, 22
   retirement of, 24
   and Rookie of the Year, 21
   statistics, 27
Robinson, Jerry (father), 5
Robinson, Mack (brother), 8
Robinson, Mallie (mother), 4–5, 6, 7
Robinson, Rachel Isum (wife), 9, 11, 17, 29

segregation, 4, 10, 13–15, 22, 28
Smith, Wendell, 16

World Series, 23, 24